Discover How to Live a Purpose-Built Life

A Step-by-Step Process for Obtaining Lasting Fulfillment

Frank Perlmutter

Dedication

To Susan, Liam, Jordan, my mother, and the memory of my father.

To the people who continue to inspire me and give me the gift of purpose in my life.

Contents

Preface

I have gone down a number of life's paths at a relatively young age. I have had success along with pain, disappointment, and loss. I have had numerous roles in my life that compose my identity: son, father, husband, brother, employee, entrepreneur, CEO, volunteer, coach, and philanthropist.

At age thirty, I started a business. I needed to prove to myself that I could be successful. I aspired to make genuine relationships with people in the business world and truly help them by offering something innovative to improve their lives and to help them in their most vulnerable moments. I wanted to be a voice of unwavering integrity in what I offered and how I acted toward others. My end goal was to retire early to help animals and my eventual family and not have to work again.

I was a mixture of drive, idealism, stress, worry, happiness, anxiety, love, frustration, and exhaustion over the years. At thirty-two, I married; at thirty-three, my father passed; at thirty-seven, I had children; and at forty-six, I sold my company.

For sixteen years, I was a CEO, having built a company from scratch and accomplished my goal of selling and retiring early. Many asked me what was next—another venture where I desired more success? No, I took a different path—back to the relationships with the people with whom I wanted to spend more time—onto the collaborative ventures that gave me purpose and enjoying more of the everyday moments.

My initial goal in writing this was one of self-catharsis after I retired. Like many, I did not know how I was going to fill my time. I tried several new pursuits and revisited ones I had pushed to the side in my working years. I captured what I learned in this book, emphasizing the best principles and methods.

My Role-Identity Process (R-I Process) in the second part of my book is the primary method that brought me to a successful retirement. It clearly defined where I was, my goals, and how to get there. I use it to this day to help me identify issues and constantly improve my life. Since I delivered my first final draft of my book over three years ago, I have shared it with a number of people who have effectively used my *R-I Process* to rethink how they are living and find success.

Top-level executives and employees have discovered it helpful in finding the work they want and, more importantly, in ending the work that is unsatisfying. Many have even found the vision and justification to retire, taking the fear and uncertainty out of a difficult transition. It has been used by college students looking to have a strong foundation and vision for their future work and lives.

My book has been a living creation; I have received insightful feedback on my ideas and updated my book about fifty times! My purpose in publishing this book is to convey my experiences with my journey in the hopes that you can learn from my successes and failures—to do what you enjoy most, end both fulfilled and unsatisfying pursuits, and find purpose and satisfaction in your life right now.

Introduction

We begin our lives with a naïve purity. We interact with others to seek collaboration and friendship and validate our self-worth. As we become adults, many of us quest for success defined through wealth, fame, and power. We are taught to achieve our goals by beating and besting others.

Yet, success built on others' failures never satisfies us deep down. While many continuously drive toward success until the day they die, most of us realize that we need something more beyond money, power, and fame. We need to feel that we have made a difference. It is a purpose not found in cut-throat competition but in our collaborative relationships and helping others.

As we progress through our lives, we get a taste of many different things the world offers. It is not wrong to try them—in fact, it is very normal to do so. Experience in pleasure and pain and the growth we achieve from them is essential to get where we eventually want to be. We learn to know what feels right for us and what does not. Only then can we move on from those pursuits and people that are not right for us or that we have matured beyond and move into the roles where we achieve the greatest lasting satisfaction and self-worth.

We may not change the world in earth-shattering ways, but through everyday generous acts, we can make a meaningful difference in someone's life and in the world. We can share our knowledge and experience or help someone who may be unable to help themselves. Giving of ourselves is our way to make our lasting impression on the world—it is how we become good enough for ourselves and truly satisfied with who we are.

As we live our lives, very few of us stop to take the time to examine ourselves. Sometimes in life, we have a moment where we believe that life has passed us by. In other words, we missed something we could have enjoyed. We have gone down unsatisfying paths but mindlessly kept going and going. If we would have paused to self-reflect, we could have made adjustments.

While we may not realize it, there is a time limit for enjoying the people and activities that bring value to our lives. People move on or pass away. We become physically unable to do demanding or even everyday activities. Later in life, many are fraught with regret—in relationships we wish we would have had and in adventures we wish we would have pursued.

It is crucial *now* to be the people we want to be and build our relationships and pursuits around that. We must understand the motivations for our actions to evaluate if we are the type of

The Four Approaches to Life

Our motivations, goals, and life perspectives shape our approaches to (or phases of) life. We perform actions to achieve our goals. Most of our actions involve interactions with others—with family, classmates, co-workers, fellow participants in joint pursuits (e.g., sports teams, hobbies, etc.), and strangers. I have identified four approaches or phases to or of life in Exhibit A. We typically go through each of these phases chronologically.

Exhibit A: The Four Approaches to Life

Personal Motivations/Goals	Typical Period in (U.S.) Life
APPROACH OR PHASE I: COLLABORATIVE AND EXPLORATORY	
<ul><li>Discover what we enjoy and what we do not.</li><li>Feel good about ourselves, validated by people liking us.</li><li>Desire to be treated fairly.</li></ul>	Before competitive sports and school with grades, competition is being introduced at a young age, limiting the time in this phase.
APPROACH OR PHASE II: COMPETITIVE AND SUCCESS-DRIVEN	
<ul><li>Prove to ourselves that our abilities are good enough.</li><li>Want to be successful, proven by amassing wealth, fame, promotions, grades, awards, and winning any competitive activity.</li></ul>	Begins when competition starts, typically in sports or school, and continues throughout most or all our working lives.
APPROACH OR PHASE III: SELF-REFLECTIVE	
<ul><li>Feeling unfulfilled but do not know why.</li><li>Wanting more in life than what success is giving us.</li><li>Regret that we are missing out on meaningful relationships and life pursuits.</li></ul>	Mid-life or later
APPROACH OR PHASE IV: COLLABORATIVE AND PURPOSEFUL	
<ul><li>Desire to have a purpose in life.</li><li>Desire to make a meaningful difference in the world.</li><li>Realization that self-satisfaction is achieved via working with others, not against them.</li></ul>	Retirement to end-of-life

In the first approach or phase as young children, we have an innate desire to want to be good people, make relationships with others, and explore the world while being treated fairly by others. The second approach or phase is where we learn to be competitive and seek success by being better than and having more than other people. The third approach or phase is one where we reach a point of reflection, wondering why we do not feel as fulfilled as we once had been. We regret that we are missing out on our relationships and realize that our approach to the world via an always competitive-driven life cannot be permanently satisfying. Our final approach or phase is driven by our desire to reconnect with our collaborative relationships and have a greater purpose in our lives.

Exhibit A provides us with several important insights:

- **We are taught to be competitive at a young age.**

- **We spend the great majority of our life seeking success (in Approach or Phase II).**

- **We become self-reflective because we are unsatisfied.**

- **Our destination goal (Approach or Phase IV) is the same one we started with (Approach or Phase I): being collaborative.**

- **We postpone being collaborative (again) and seeking purpose until later in life.**

Living a life like this is not ideal. Where we start and end up is the same—in our collaborative relationships. Yet, we spend most of our lives seeking success and eventually realize that this approach cannot provide permanent satisfaction, purpose, or happiness. In the following chapters, I will discuss these approaches or phases in detail, along with pivotal experiences in my life, insights I gained, and actionable recommendations for you. I hope that you will question the typical approach to life and carefully consider a different approach to how you live now and in the future.

Section One: An Exploration of Our Attitudes and How to Live Better

Our overall perspective of the world and how we are supposed to function in it is shaped at an early age. As children, we have an innate desire to want to be good people, make relationships with others, and explore the world. As we start to interact with others and get a sense of how the world works, we change ourselves to try to either effectively operate in it or reject it. In other words, we embrace or hate others, try to blend in or stand out, cooperate, or relentlessly compete. Common themes are taught in American society around achievement, success, working, retirement, competition, collaboration, and relationships. We are so geared toward these norms of operation and so busy and absorbed with them that we rarely stop to question whether they are suitable for us.

The point of the first section of my book is to examine our modes of operation (i.e., approaches to life) in each of the phases of our life and honestly ask ourselves if there is a better way than the typical path laid out for us. I will describe my own experiences and offer different perspectives and recommendations on how we can live our lives in what I believe is a much more fulfilling way.

people we want to be and make adjustments if we are not. We must examine and then realign ourselves.

Structure of The Book

My book is composed of two major sections. The first details how many of us live our lives and how it is less than ideal. We spend too much time seeking self-satisfaction and success and not enough time with the people and pursuits that ultimately matter in our lives—that give us meaning and purpose. This section will provide you with thought-provoking ways to live your life differently by questioning the societal definition and value of success, providing ways for self-reflection, and understanding how fulfilling a purposeful life can be.

The second section of my book details a method I developed for self-examination called *The Role-Identity (R-I) Process*. We are composed of individual roles that collectively make up our identity. We have collaborative, self-centered, life-sustaining, and passive roles. Some provide us with satisfaction and improve our self-worth, others take away from it, while others have no effect at all.

You can use the book's first section to provide a perspective of how you want to live your life. You can then use *The R-I Process* to understand the composition of your current identity, where you spend your time, and how much each role in your life contributes to your positive identity. You continue by defining your ideal future identity, composed of roles that will maximize your satisfaction in life. Finally, you construct a plan to reach your goals and then continually monitor yourself and adjust as you move forward.

My book is intended to make a difference in your life by offering you a new perspective on how to look at yourself and providing a proven method to get where you want to be. I anticipate my thoughts and my *R-I Process* will evolve. So, stay tuned for discoveries, updates, and stories as we all move forward!

Living a life like this is not ideal. Where we start and end up is the same—in our collaborative relationships. Yet, we spend most of our lives seeking success and eventually realize that this approach cannot provide permanent satisfaction, purpose, or happiness. In the following chapters, I will discuss these approaches or phases in detail, along with pivotal experiences in my life, insights I gained, and actionable recommendations for you. I hope that you will question the typical approach to life and carefully consider a different approach to how you live now and in the future.

In the first approach or phase as young children, we have an innate desire to want to be good people, make relationships with others, and explore the world while being treated fairly by others. The second approach or phase is where we learn to be competitive and seek success by being better than and having more than other people. The third approach or phase is one where we reach a point of reflection, wondering why we do not feel as fulfilled as we once had been. We regret that we are missing out on our relationships and realize that our approach to the world via an always competitive-driven life cannot be permanently satisfying. Our final approach or phase is driven by our desire to reconnect with our collaborative relationships and have a greater purpose in our lives.

Exhibit A provides us with several important insights:

- **We are taught to be competitive at a young age.**

- **We spend the great majority of our life seeking success (in Approach or Phase II).**

- **We become self-reflective because we are unsatisfied.**

- **Our destination goal (Approach or Phase IV) is the same one we started with (Approach or Phase I): being collaborative.**

- **We postpone being collaborative (again) and seeking purpose until later in life.**

Exhibit A: The Four Approaches to Life

Personal Motivations/Goals	Typical Period in (U.S.) Life
APPROACH OR PHASE I: COLLABORATIVE AND EXPLORATORY	
<ul><li>Discover what we enjoy and what we do not.</li><li>Feel good about ourselves, validated by people liking us.</li><li>Desire to be treated fairly.</li></ul>	Before competitive sports and school with grades, competition is being introduced at a young age, limiting the time in this phase.
APPROACH OR PHASE II: COMPETITIVE AND SUCCESS-DRIVEN	
<ul><li>Prove to ourselves that our abilities are good enough.</li><li>Want to be successful, proven by amassing wealth, fame, promotions, grades, awards, and winning any competitive activity.</li></ul>	Begins when competition starts, typically in sports or school, and continues throughout most or all our working lives.
APPROACH OR PHASE III: SELF-REFLECTIVE	
<ul><li>Feeling unfulfilled but do not know why.</li><li>Wanting more in life than what success is giving us.</li><li>Regret that we are missing out on meaningful relationships and life pursuits.</li></ul>	Mid-life or later
APPROACH OR PHASE IV: COLLABORATIVE AND PURPOSEFUL	
<ul><li>Desire to have a purpose in life.</li><li>Desire to make a meaningful difference in the world.</li><li>Realization that self-satisfaction is achieved via working with others, not against them.</li></ul>	Retirement to end-of-life

The Four Approaches to Life

Our motivations, goals, and life perspectives shape our approaches to (or phases of) life. We perform actions to achieve our goals. Most of our actions involve interactions with others—with family, classmates, co-workers, fellow participants in joint pursuits (e.g., sports teams, hobbies, etc.), and strangers. I have identified four approaches or phases to or of life in Exhibit A. We typically go through each of these phases chronologically.

Chapter Two

Approach or Phase I: Pure: Wanting Fairness and Goodness

We are born pure with an innate trust in others. We believe the world is a good and fair place where people look out for each other. As children, we seek to be collaborative and make friends. We want to be good people, feel appreciated, and explore what the world offers. There are experiences via our interactions with others that can drive us to either reject or embrace people in the world. Let's examine each of them below and see how we can form a better path.

An Almost Immediate Erosion of Trust in Others

When we care about people, it leaves us vulnerable to disappointment, rejection, and pain. Some people will inevitably treat us poorly or unfairly. When this happens, it is natural to shield ourselves from—or altogether avoid—those people. For this reason, children often only trust a few people or nobody at all. Relationships are not met with openness but skepticism, and new relationships are not sought.

Many children protect themselves by seeking competition. The reason they do this is because competition accomplishes two goals: punishing others who will inevitably hurt us and winning so that we feel good about ourselves. Healthy competition certainly makes us better. We compete, learn, enjoy the experience, and are collaborative again after the competition. However, more often than not, our competitive nature forces an approach where someone else has to punitively lose for us to win. Even worse, in many, it encourages a win-by-any-means attitude, whereby selfishness, revenge, a lack of forgiveness, and cheating are somehow justified.

As parents, coaches, and mentors, we can encourage a positive approach to the competition by facilitating learning and passion while strongly emphasizing that a win-by-any-means approach is never acceptable.

Learning From the Pain but Staying Collaborative

It is natural to shield ourselves and our children from pain. However, pain is an inevitable part of life and growth; it is essential that we feel it and build ourselves to be resilient in the face of it. When I was young, I learned the pain of discrimination, betrayal, abandonment, and rejection—some from those I thought were my friends and some who were strangers. I was upset, angry, and disappointed in many people.

However, there were just as many people who weren't that way to me—people who were friendly and others who were struggling like me. There was a constant decision on whether I wanted to hate the world or keep trying to find good friends—to be vengeful or be forgiving. Through the pain, I grew. My family and friends supported me as I became resilient. I made relationships with people I still have to this day. They support me and love me, and I them.

If we never fail or feel pain, we will never know how to deal with it. If we always demand to win and never fail, we will never mature. We will be stuck, upset, and angry whenever something doesn't go our way. Through pain, I learned patience, hard work, and tolerance for others. Pain does not last forever unless we let it. We must experience it, learn from it, move on, and continually search for those truly collaborative and meaningful relationships.

Chapter Three

Approach or Phase II: Competitive and Seeking Success

We have an internal conflict between wanting to be and do good and our desire to get our fair share, feel appreciated, and be successful. When these two desires are at odds, we sometimes violate our values to get what we believe we deserve.

There is an appetite that starts in our youth to find out how far our ability will take us. We measure our abilities versus others through competition—grades, game scores, and awards. As adults, we competitively measure our success via wealth, fame, and power. We believe our self-worth is predicated upon these measures and incorporate pursuits of achievement as the primary part of our lives. We also think that the more successful we are, the more value we have to others and the world. However, this is frequently the opposite case, as our success often requires the personal failure of others.

Competitive vs. Collaborative: Coaching Recreational Children's Sports

Coaching my kids at recreational and intramural team sports is a role that has been a big part of my life. Over the years, I have fixated on doing it the right way and always having fun. I am teaching children not just the sport but teamwork and sportsmanship principles—the proper way to act and to treat others. I noticed over the years that I didn't get horribly upset at losing or terribly excited about winning. Yes, I was happy or disappointed, but it wasn't an extreme feeling either way.

However, I was greatly affected by how the children reacted to others during and after the game, how they and the other children played the game, whether there was an overall sense of fairness to the game, and the attitudes of the other coaches. Did the coaches (including me) have integrity, play all the kids, and want their players to have fun, or were they consumed with winning at any cost? My attitude toward coaching my children's team really forced me to examine myself to see why I got so upset about some things while I was very passive about winning or losing.

I found my answers by asking my kids some questions. They told me that their favorite teams were the ones where they felt the closest and had the most fun with their teammates. They described times of winning championships and being miserable or losing most of their games yet being elated. They asked if I noticed how they didn't care much about a win or loss; they didn't even bring it up the next day. They were wholly focused on making connections with others and a sense that they were provided an equitable playing field. They brought up wonderful plays and teammates and bemoaned the times when the integrity of coaches, players, and referees was questionable to them. I saw that the competition was about collaboration, and they weren't willing to compromise their integrity to win.

It made me contemplate not only how to coach but if I and others were willing to make the same commitment to integrity in our everyday lives. Was it possible to live with ourselves if we lost? Could we continue to accept some losing outcomes, or would we succumb to taking shortcuts to win at the cost of compromising our integrity? Most importantly for the kids, what were we teaching them about how to approach life, and what was most important? Did our actions drive away a potential for collaboration for the sake of a fleeting win or a quickly forgotten loss?

Putting Success in Perspective

When we seek success and achieve it, in that moment, we prove that we are good enough for ourselves in the world. To feel we are permanently good enough for ourselves, we have to answer this question,

"How much money, fame, or power do I need, or how many times do I need to win before I am completely satisfied?"

When we think about that question, we realize it is almost impossible to answer. One big reason it is so difficult to answer is that there is no universally accepted definition of success. Without a universally or widely accepted definition, it isn't easy to define a goal or a finish line where we would stop questing for success. Without ever being completely satisfied, many of us will continually raise the bar for our success and never stop pursuing it. It is challenging to stop seeking our subsequent success voluntarily without a finish line.

Even worse, our quest for success typically stops when we are forced to stop (not voluntarily stop). We lose our jobs, get forced to retire, get sick, or die.

This is truly a sad state of affairs. Let's examine our approaches to life (from Exhibit A) with ages, time, and life percentages spent in each one:

Exhibit B: The Four Approaches to Life with Ages, Time, % of Life

Approach to Life	Typical Start Age	Typical Finish Age	Duration (in Years)	% of Life
I: Collaborative/Exploratory	Birth	10-13	10-13	13%-17%
II: Competitive	11-14	59-70	45-59	59%-77%
III: Self-Reflective	N/A	N/A	N/A	N/A
IV: Collaborative/Purposeful	60-71	76.4	5.4-16.4	7%-21%

Please note: This chart is based on a (2021) average U.S. Life Expectancy of 76.4 years.
Source: Centers for Disease Control & Prevention

We spend most of our life in Phase II pursuing success: 59%-77% of it!

We eventually are self-reflective (Phase III) and return to the collaboration that we sought in our childhood. Still, phase IV is typically very short (only 7%-21%) and occurs when we are older. We may not be able to enjoy those more senior years as much as we would have enjoyed our younger ones.

Most people would agree that the purpose of work is to have enough money, not to work for the sake of working. If we find our work collaborative, meaningful, and purposeful that is a wonderful situation which should be enjoyed as long as possible. However, many find work as a means to an end with the goal of having enough money to retire so that we can spend more time with the people and pursuits we love and enjoy in Phase IV. Based on that, it would make sense to get to Phase IV as quickly as possible, minimizing the time we spend in Phase II.

My point is not that we should entirely skip a quest for success but that we should put it in a different perspective. We should view it as a temporary stop along life's journey that composes a fraction, not the majority of our lives. We eventually mature and grow out of the desire to achieve individually and go back to our collaborative relationships and pursuits.

Additionally, we tend to lose sight of our relationships as we get older. We sideline them or forget about them entirely as we work. We also lose sight of the big picture of having purpose in our lives as the days go by quickly and unquestioned. We do not become self-reflective (Phase III) until Phase II becomes unbearable.

Suppose we recognize this situation earlier in life. In that case, we can be persistently self-reflective and realize that it makes sense to never lose sight of our collaborative relationships as the ultimate goal. We can be successful and savor those times of personal success, but always keep our relationships and collaborative pursuits as a core focus of our lives.

So, to make success a temporary stop (i.e., to end Phase II), we need to answer the difficult question, *"How much success is enough?"*

We can do this by understanding the overall value of success to our self-worth, setting finish lines (i.e., goals), and moving on when we are done.

Wealth: Determining How Much is Enough Money

Let's take a closer look at our pursuit of wealth. Almost all of us need to work to make a living. Making a living is having enough for our core living expenses (rent or mortgage, transportation, etc.) plus money that we can use for the things we want (also known as discretionary expenses). Having enough money to live is our first goal.

Once we understand our core living expenses, we look at our future (and more significant) expenses. The future may have more considerable expenses that require substantial amounts of cash or the ability to borrow money via a loan or credit. Some examples of these expenses are a child's education, a house, or a car. Once we have purchased those items, our future costs typically significantly decrease. After we make these purchases, future ones are for what we want, not what we need. Therefore, with some willpower, we can reduce those costs.

Determining how much we really need must be done via a detailed calculation. However, as I have found with most people, they guess how much they need to make or save and what their future and current expenses are. Additionally, when they did guess what they needed later in life, they typically grossly overestimated the cost (e.g., college for a child is $2 million!).

Simply put, we have to write it down and use an objective calculation in this all-important exercise. We also need to have the correct information on the significant expenses, not a guess. (Please refer to Appendix A for more details on how I developed a financial spreadsheet to document this information.)

The other critical item to examine (and balance) with money is time. Most never consider how long it would take to reach their monetary goal to retire. Let's define retirement as a factor of work and money—**when we have enough money to fulfill our future money goals, we stop working!**

In using my spreadsheet with my mentees and entering in the monetary amounts they thought they needed to retire, I saw retirement ages ranging from 75 to over 130 years old! Obviously, these were unrealistic. It was easy to understand why they thought they would be working the rest of their lives. When we see these numbers, we immediately realize we must determine a financial goal that is realistic and attainable within a reasonable amount of time. We MUST balance money with time (to retirement).

Documenting these numbers in my financial spreadsheet provided me with a clear goal and a timeline. I was also able to have calculated numbers instead of guesses on how much big-ticket items like college tuition and a house cost. I gained insights into expenses that were too high or unnecessary so I could proactively reduce them.

My biggest lessons learned about money are:

- Write it down! It's too important to guess and do calculations in your head!

- Stop working when you have enough money.

- Stick with your calculations and your finish line. Do not keep increasing your goal when you have attained it. If you do, you will just keep working and working.

- Do not trade away precious time with family, friends, and pursuits for the ability to make more money than your finish line goal.

- Examine how you can spend less time on work and more time with family, friends, and pursuits NOW!

A Deeper Examination of Fame and Power

Fame and power bring us attention and influence over others. In the moments when others are praising us and providing us with adoration, we feel good about ourselves.

When I started my company, I worked tirelessly in my basement. I sacrificed my time and did not take any salary for four years. I traveled relentlessly to give as many talks and meet as many people as I could so that I could create awareness to grow my business. It worked. The company grew, as well as my notoriety. I won numerous awards and spoke all over the world. I was the president of a small company who became the CEO of a large company in a small industry with more and more employees. My company's success was a validation of my hard work. My clients were happy and appreciated what I had done for them, which was a validation of my sacrifice.

I continued to speak, win awards, and get more clients. However, with each passing moment of fame and power, I wasn't getting the satisfaction that I used to. Moments were fleeting, not permanent. With more clients, speaking, and traveling, more and more of my total time was exhausted. My life was that of a CEO first. That was the prime role that composed most of my identity. Although I was a father, friend, spouse, son, coach, and volunteer, most of my time and thoughts were spent on my business.

I reached moments of self-examination. When I thought about my work, I asked myself and answered several essential questions:

- How many more talks would I have to do, and how many more awards would I need to win to feel satisfied? **There was no answer to this question! I would just keep doing presentations and aspiring to win more awards.**

- Did I accomplish my original goal of providing something to the industry and the world that helped others? **The answer was most definitely "Yes!" However, I accomplished that goal years ago. I was in a cycle of surrendering my valuable time to revalidate that success again and again.**

- Based on my retirement calculation in my spreadsheet, did I have enough money to retire? **The answer was also "Yes."**

Through my journey, I learned a number of essential lessons about fame and power:

- They provide temporary validation that we are good enough, but not lasting satisfaction.

- They are for the benefit of ourselves (self-centered), not for the benefit of others.

- Our competitive nature can drive us to try to beat those with more power or fame. Someone will always have more fame or power than us; that puts us on a never-ending quest.

- Fame and power are difficult to quantify, making it difficult to know when we have had enough of them to stop pursuing them and move on.

- As our fame and notoriety grow, our privacy diminishes.

Knowing the drawbacks of fame and power, we may decide that we do not want them or stop seeking them. If they are a part of our lives, we must realize that they can be all-absorbing for us. It is not wrong to have a taste of any of them but to feel true satisfaction in our lives, we need to treat them as phases, as fleeting pleasures to be enjoyed and then left behind as fond memories. We realize that it is nice to experience these things, but it should always be our goal to move past them and onto what is truly satisfying—lasting purpose in our lives.

Chapter Four

Approach or Phase III: Self-Reflection and Making a Voluntary Change

S elf-reflection is typically a phase in our lives that arrives when we realize that success is no longer satisfying. Let's take a look at what typically happens.

It is not easy to stop working or to work less. I can honestly say this from personal experience! Since my business was very successful, I was running fast. I ignored the finish line and just kept on running. In my head and my heart, I felt I was completely justified. I needed more money for my family (I didn't—I had met my goal). My clients really needed me (they didn't—others could help them). My employees needed my guidance so I couldn't leave (they didn't, they were very talented).

The primary reason I kept working was that I was scared to move on after doing my job for over fifteen years. Even though I was frustrated, tired, stressed, and unhealthy, I ignored those and kept going until I could not do it anymore. It took a concussion to stop me cold and force an honest examination of how I was living my life. I had to spend two weeks alone, in the dark, left with my thoughts. It took months for my head to stop hurting, but in my moments of clarity, I realized that it was time to stop my quest for success and move on to the next phase of my life. It was time for me to spend time with the people I loved and pursuits I always wanted to do instead of working.

I wasn't forced into retirement, but I was forced to look at myself very carefully. It is a shame to be forced into something, especially if unprepared. Getting to the next phase of our lives should be voluntary.

One interesting statistic is that on average people retire five years earlier than they expect— at sixty-one versus a sixty-six-year-old expectation![1]

---

1. 7/22/2022 Gallup Economy and Personal Finance Survey. Expected Retirement Age vs. Actual Retirement Age data has been gathered for the last 20 years. In every year of the survey, Actual Retirement Age has been younger than Expected Retirement Age!

As I mentioned earlier, our pursuit of success typically stops when we are forced to stop. We generally are unprepared to retire earlier than expected; we have no plan for how we will live our lives. Yet, having a comprehensive plan is absolutely critical to our lives. It shows our finish lines, where we hope to be next, and the steps required to get there.

We do not need to wait to examine our lives. It is much better to reflect constantly on our lives than to have a moment of grand self-reflection forced upon us. Self-reflection should not be a phase but rather something we should be doing throughout our lives. There is no wrong time to examine ourselves, evaluate our satisfaction, and make adjustments. It is also never too late to self-reflect, even if we failed to do so earlier in life.

Methods of Self-Reflection to Move Beyond a Success-Driven Approach

Reflect on Our Original Purpose of Work

A great way to self-reflect (and move on) is to examine the original reasons and the current reasons why we work. I thought about my original reasons and goals when I started my business and asked myself whether I had achieved them. My professional goal was to improve the lives of professionals like me by correcting the unfair and unhelpful practices in my industry. My personal goal was to make enough money to provide a wonderful life for my family and give back to the animal welfare community that had provided so much to me.

I made substantial positive changes to the industry through my software, intellectual property, and training. I helped thousands of people like me. I also had enough money to support my family. I had reached my goals. As I said above, when we have reached our goals, there is nothing left to achieve. It is time to stop pursuing success and move on to the next phase of our lives.

Review Work Time vs. Collaborative Time

Another motivation to stop seeking competitive success is to reflect upon the time we spend at work (or unconsciously thinking about it) versus the amount of conscious time we spend with our family, friends, and other pursuits. We have times during the day when we are at our best—when our brains are active, thoughtful, and aware. We have other times when we are tired and mindlessly doing tasks to get through the day.

I always found that I was best from around 8:30 am to 3 pm. So, about six and a half hours out of the day. All of those hours were dedicated to working. Outside of those hours, I was sometimes either tired, moody, or both. The best of me was not always present during those off-hours. Those were the hours when I spent time with my family and friends, and they were sometimes not getting the best part of me. That motivated me to consider how I could restructure my days, how I could work less, and ultimately, how I could stop working altogether.

Envision the Likelihood to Maintain Relationships & Ability to Perform Current Activities Later in Life

The main goal of working is to support those we love, but we give up precious time with them to work. We trade our present time for supposed future time with them. We trade time in our prime for time in our older age. We trade time with our children for time with them when they are adults.

When we unconsciously make this trade, we hope that we do not become infirm, sick, or die and that our relationships have not eroded before we reach that wonderful time to enjoy them. As I have discussed, that is typically not a good bet. Relationships are nurtured and grow by spending time with others. Suppose we did not dedicate time to our relationships with family and friends in our working years. In that case, there is a high probability that those relationships will be gone or highly damaged when we eventually try to go back to them. We must thoughtfully consider the trade-off between time now with loved ones and our pursuit of wealth, fame, and power. We must continuously ask ourselves the question, *"Is this pursuit worth the time that I will be surrendering with the people who I love?"*

Another way to self-reflect is to think about our age and what we are currently able to do physically and mentally. Then, think about what we will be able to do when we retire.

Answer the questions, *"What activities that I currently enjoy won't I be able to do or enjoy as much?"* and *"Is it worth me trading my time to work instead of doing those activities now?"*

One life-changing moment for me was with my father. I had a fantastic relationship with him. He was healthy up until the age of sixty-one when he was diagnosed with stage IV pancreatic cancer. I had gotten married a month and a half before his diagnosis. After he was diagnosed and started experimental treatments and chemotherapy, he still insisted on going to work. He did that until he could barely move or even eat because of the pain. He died eight months after his diagnosis.

If you remember, sixty-one is the average actual retirement age. My dad never stopped caring for others, being generous, and joking around. However, he missed out entirely on what was supposed to be his retirement. I have known a number of people who have lost family and friends at a young age. It is truly a motivating factor not to wait to self-reflect and to do all you can to enjoy your time now with the people that you love and the pursuits about which you are passionate.

The last and most thorough method of self-reflection was a method I built called *The Role-Identity (R-I) Process*. I will discuss this in detail in the next section of my book.

Chapter Five

Approach or Phase IV: Purposeful and Helping Others

A Purpose-Built Mindset

What is your purpose? In other words, what brings meaning to your life?

We need to find purpose in our lives. Our purpose comes from making a difference in the world—that it is a better place for having us here. When we help others, we feel that we are making a difference. We need to feel useful in and to the world—important, essential, and valuable to the people in it. We can only be useful to the world when it is for others, not for ourselves.

Our lives are about filling our days with moments that gratify us. It revolves around having relationships where we can love and be loved. We should be spending time with our loved ones instead of rushing back to do work. It is critical to make the time to enjoy others rather than postponing, missing out, or waiting to get around to those moments. Ultimately, we must stop our need to accomplish and redistribute ourselves to the roles that give us the time to enjoy life.

You do not need to boil the ocean to make a difference and reach your goal of being purposeful. Finding purpose is not as difficult as you think. When someone reaches out to you for help, it is an opportunity for you. If there is not someone for you to help, keep looking. Those who need your advice, time, money, etc., are not hard to find. Finding a person or cause about which you feel passionate may take some time, but be patient. It will ultimately complete you and fill in the spaces previously occupied by the competitive roles you had. It will make you feel that you are good enough.

To have had a positive effect on someone else is the most satisfying, most incredible way to make your impression on the world. Those gifts will continue long after you are gone, as others learn from you and continue your good ways.

Making a Major Life Transition

Major life transitions happen when we have a major shift in our roles. Some examples of major life transitions are living on your own, starting a job, getting married, having a child, and retirement. Major life transitions are challenging but can be made easier if we plan for them.

Before I sold my company, I made a decision that I did not want to be the CEO anymore. I only committed to being an advisor for a year and then would resign from the company altogether. I knowingly made this decision and knew it would take time to get used to since I was effectively eliminating 70% of my current roles (the self-centered, work-related ones) and needed to find other roles to fill the void that would be left in my identity. I knew I wanted to spend more time with family and friends and volunteer. However, I wasn't sure if I could make a full-time life out of those relationships and pursuits without work. Some of my biggest fears were the uncertainty whether my new roles would be fulfilling, if I would feel good about myself, and if I would have enough to do.

I can equate my eighteen months after the sale of my company as akin to an extreme withdrawal. I still wanted to be involved, make decisions, help clients, and correct mistakes. Working and driving decisions were in my nature; work had been my primary source of validation for sixteen years, and it was gone. That period was about me weaning myself off work and my success-driven mindset. It was a time of learning to be enough for the world (and myself) in a different way. A critical moment of realization for me that helped in my transition was that I had always stayed in my collaborative roles when I was working. I was also gradually (and unconsciously) moving back to my collaborative roles because I wanted to spend more time in them and less time in my work roles. The goal was not to stay busy but to find meaningful ways to find purpose in my life through collaborative pursuits. That period of time was initially rough, but gradually got better and then wonderful as I explored more and more collaborative roles, both old and new.

I had a plan (as per my R-I Process) and executed on it. I focused on spending more meaningful time with my family and friends. What I found was that even though I was eager and able to make the change and come up with new activities, family and friends were not as aligned with those activities and time commitments as I was, due to them still working. I desired a deeper connection with them and told them that even though I knew we could not dedicate the same amount of time, I wanted to do something that would take us past our routine of periodic phone calls and rare meetings. I remembered how we had connected in the past and discussed this and my concerns about us growing apart. Together, we made plans to see each other more often and set times on our calendars that took priority over any self-centered role activity. This had a fantastic positive effect.

We also need pursuits outside of our family and friends. I rekindled my passions for helping animals and philanthropy by starting a charitable fund and joining a foundation board that supports nonprofits that help others prepare for and recover from disasters. I started writing (this book), joined a band, and continued to coach.

I started mentoring others to share what I had learned over the years, giving them professional advice, helping them find new jobs, and giving them personal advice. It has been a fantastic feeling when they have found new jobs or realized a new pathway in their lives from my advice. They have helped me, too, in knowing that I can still make a difference and that they value me. I find true satisfaction and purpose in mentoring, supporting and collaborating with others who are finding their way in the world and are dedicated to making a difference. I genuinely appreciate the sharing over the receiving.

Fundamental to moving forward was the idea of building a *Purpose-Built* life instead of a *Success-Driven* one. A *Purpose-Built* life focuses on collaboration and getting satisfaction through helping others while a *Success-Driven* life focuses on competition and achievements. When we reach this phase, our attitudes have genuinely matured. Ironically enough, we have made a full circle back to our childhood. We are once again eager to explore the world we haven't had time to discover, and we desire to have meaningful, lasting relationships for the rest of our lives.

Section 2: The Role-Identity (R-I) Process

We understand how important it is to spend time with the people we love and on the pursuits in which we find purpose. Ongoing self-reflection and evaluation are essential processes to understand where we are in our journey—assessing whether or not we are on the right path and making needed changes.

To become who we want to be, we must first understand ourselves. We are complex— influenced by a myriad of different, frequently conflicting roles that we occupy in our lives. Some examples of roles are parent, friend, and volunteer. Other roles in our lives are those we associate with characteristics or traits in us or that we desire to have, like intelligence, health, and wealth. Taken together, our roles collectively compose our identity—who we are as a total person.

When we look at the roles that compose our identity, we get a detailed picture of the path we are on in life. We can see whether we emphasize collaborative roles like family and friends or competitive roles that focus on wealth and power. We can identify passive, time-consuming roles like performing chores. We can pinpoint the roles that bring us the greatest satisfaction and those that do little or nothing for us at all.

We can map our future identity with more or less time dedicated to our current roles, along with new ones that we believe will bring us greater satisfaction. By documenting this, we can gain an understanding of who we are and who we want to be as people. Developing a plan to get there is the key step to reaching our goals.

To understand the roles in my life and how they influenced my identity, I developed *The Role-Identity (R-I) Process.* Via this process, we can gain insights and make adjustments to live the life we want now and create a path for who we want to be. The R-I Process is broken down into four parts, with steps in each one:

- Current Role-Identity (R-I) Mapping

- Future Role-Identity (R-I)Mapping

- Role-Identity (R-I) Action Planning

- Role-Identity (R-I) Evaluation and Monitoring

Chapter Six

Part I: Current Role-Identity (R-I) Mapping

Current Role-Identity (R-I) Mapping is the first part of the R-I Process. It is where we document our roles, put them into categories, and define how much each contributes to our positive identity and self-worth.

Step 1: Define and Classify the Roles that Compose Your Identity

The first step in Current R-I Mapping is documenting the roles that compose your identity and classifying each as a Role Type. There are four different role types:

- **Collaborative**: Collaborative roles are defined as roles where we help or work with others for a greater purpose. Our typical collaborative roles are family ones like parent, child, and sibling. Some other examples of roles where we help or work with people for the greater good are mentor, coach, and volunteer.

- **Self-Centered**: Self-centered roles are defined as roles where the benefit is for ourselves, not for others. These are typically our (Phase II) success-driven or work roles.

- **Life-Supporting:** Life-Supporting roles provide the necessary support for our other roles. We need to be physically, mentally, and emotionally able to perform our other roles. We also need enough money to be able to live. Roles at work and around physical or mental fitness can be both life-supporting and self-centered. In other words, there is a point at which they go beyond self-sustaining and become self-centered. For example, we work to have enough money to live (life-supporting role). It becomes a self-centered role when we surpass that to amass wealth beyond what we need (taking time away from our collaborative roles). I capture the life-supporting role of "what I need" as one role (e.g., wage earner) and the self-centered role of "what I want" (e.g., wealthy person) as a second role.

- **Passive:** Passive roles are neither collaborative nor competitive. These are roles that have to be done, like chores, food shopping, or driving to work.

Some roles can be any of the types. It depends on what purpose the role plays in our identity. For example, roles that some consider collaborative, like attending religious services, may be seen as passive because they seem like a chore. Also, some people find great pleasure in doing chores since the routine calms or grounds them, while some view chores as mundane or cumbersome. Here are some examples of the roles that we may include in our Current R-I Mapping:

- Parent
- Son/Daughter
- Brother/Sister
- Friend

- Employee
- Business Owner

- Coach
- Mentor
- Neighbor
- Shopper
- Driver/Commuter
- Philanthropist
- Sports Player
- Knowledge Seeker

- Educator
- Volunteer
- Adventurer
- Financially Responsible Person
- Caretaker
- Egalitarian/Social Justice Seeker
- Role Model
- Healthy Person
- Mindful Person
- Modest Person
- Gamer
- Famous Person
- Financially Successful Person
- Powerful Person

You can use the Role List worksheet in Appendix C to capture your Current Roles.

Step 2: Define How Much Each Role Currently Contributes to Your Positive Identity

Our self-worth (positive identity) is influenced by the roles we perform in life. Each role contributes to our positive identity. The next step is documenting a percentage that each contributes to your positive identity, with the role percentages totaling 100%. Really think about where you derive the most satisfaction and self-worth. Ensure that you are documenting the level of satisfaction rather than the time spent on the role. One may spend many hours in a role that delivers little or no satisfaction. In the next step, you will document how much time you spend in each of your roles.

Step 3: Capture How Much Time You Spend in Each Role

Now, we are going to examine our roles quantitatively, where we document how much time we spend **doing or thinking** about each. Our thinking time is essential to consider. There are times when we may be performing one role, like being a parent but thinking about another role, like an employee. Another example is that we may be trying to sleep, but we are worrying about work. Our brains control our feelings and, ultimately, our identity. While we may be physically in one place, our thoughts may be focused on another. Time is, therefore, allocated to the role we are thinking about at the time rather than the one we are physically doing.

In this step, capture the time spent on your thoughts. You do not have to be exact; the vital part is documenting it. If you want to get more precise, there are time-keeping apps and software tools that can do this almost automatically for you. You enter the role name and then click the timer when you start and then when you finish.

As I mentioned before, with work, we typically have several roles. The Life-Supporting role is the Wage Earner Role. There is a point in which the amount of money you earn becomes more than what you need. In your Wage Earner Role, document your total time at work and your percentage earning what you need. Anything earned in excess of what you need will go into a self-centered role, Wealthy Person.

Exhibit C: Current Role-Identity Mapping Worksheet

STEP 1	STEP 2	STEP 3
Role in Life	% Current Contribution to Positive Identity	% Time Spent
Collaborative Roles		
Parent	15%	7%
Spouse	10%	3%
Friend	10%	3%
Child	6%	2%
Brother	4%	1%
Coach	3%	3%
Volunteer	7%	1%
Self-Centered Roles		
Industry (Famous/Powerful) Leader	10%	15%
Wealthy Person	10%	25%
Beautiful Person	10%	15%
Life-Supporting Roles		
Wage Earner	5%	10%
Hygienic Person	5%	1%
Mentally/Emotionally Stable Person	5%	1%
Passive Roles		
Commuter	0%	4%
Chore Provider	0%	7%
Shopper	0%	6%
	100%	100%
TOTAL Collaborative	*55%*	*21%*
TOTAL Self-Centered	*30%*	*50%*
TOTAL Life-Supporting	*15%*	*12%*
TOTAL Passive	*0%*	*17%*

You can use the Current R-I Mapping, Future R-I Mapping, and Role Identity Action Planning Worksheet in Appendix C to capture Percentage Current Contribution to Positive Identity and Percentage of Time Spent in each role.

Chapter Seven

Part II: Future Role-Identity (R-I) Mapping

With Future Role-Identity (R-I) Mapping, we map the identity of the person we want to be. It starts with establishing an overall direction for ourselves. We do this by first setting percentage targets categorically (i.e., collaborative, self-centered, life-supporting, and passive). Then, individual roles are examined for possible changes.

Step 4: Establish an Overall Future Direction for Yourself

As we review our Current R-I Mapping, we typically realize that we have issues with our role contributions to identity and allocations of time spent among roles. Our collaborative roles (from which we get the most satisfaction) may be neglected, diminished, or ignored. Our self-centered and passive roles may be absorbing the great majority or our identity. As I described in the first section of my book, it is no surprise that we find that the roles in which we spend the great majority of our time fail to deliver us satisfaction or purpose.

Knowing how we want to live our lives is the first step in making a change. Via the following grid, let's re-examine the different types of roles and how we may want them in our lives. You will capture a core aim, a target percentage, and guiding principles for each role type. The target percentage is both the percentage of self-worth you hope to derive and the amount of time you ideally want to spend in that category. You are aligning your goals with what you want your reality to be. To document this, you may want to use the example chart in Exhibit D or compose your own.

Exhibit D: Future Role Identity Mapping Worksheet

Role Category	Core Aim	Target %
Collaborative	Achieve true contentment by providing something of value to the world by helping others	75%

Guiding Principles:

- Focus your life on collaborative relationships and pursuits.
- Think about collaborative relationships and pursuits you had earlier in your life and explore reincorporating them back into your identity.
- Do not postpone or eliminate your collaborative roles; special moments are missed and cannot be revisited, and relationships are frequently damaged or lost.
- Maintain collaborative roles throughout your entire life.
- You may not be able to change the world vastly, but you certainly can through everyday moments of giving.
- Someone can always use your help. Seek out opportunities to find them.

Role Category	Core Aim	Target %
Self-Centered	Get a taste of success and then move on	7%

Guiding Principles:

- Set clear goals to reach and then move on from the role.
- Pleasure and self-worth derived from self-centered pursuits are fleeting.
- The time you spend on work-related roles is the time you are not spending with friends or family.
- Roles around fame and power are always self-centered, not for the benefit of others.
- Do not compromise your integrity to get what you want or believe you deserve. There is never any satisfaction when success comes from cheating.
- Look for ways to promote collaboration and learning while you are competing.

Exhibit D: Future Role Identity Mapping Worksheet (continued)

Role Category	Core Aim	Target %
Life-Supporting	Treat as enablers that allow you to perform other vital roles	15%

Guiding Principles:
- Work can get in the way of these roles. Be aware and do not ignore these roles.
- Health is not optional; if ignored, it will plague you throughout your life, taking your ability to perform other roles away.
- Schedule periodic appointments with health care professionals to assess current health and utilize maintenance mechanisms (e.g. physical therapy and exercise) to preserve good health.
- Utilize therapy/mental health professionals to assess current health and drive success in role-identity management.
- Like passive roles, perform these roles to a satisfactory standard. Going beyond that typically delivers little value.

Role Category	Core Aim	Target %
Passive	Complete tasks to a satisfactory standard in the least amount of time possible	3%

Guiding Principles:
- Determine ways to straight-line mundane tasks or make them more pleasurable to do.
- Do not add passive roles to your plate like social media posting, video games, or mindless web surfing.
- Do not let negative interactions with strangers bother you.

Step 5: Determine Role Treatments

Exhibit D illustrates several goals, such as a redistribution from our self-centered and passive roles into our collaborative ones. Based on our overall future direction, the next step is to evaluate each role to define whether you want them in your life more, less, or the same. You may also want to include a new role not currently in your life. This process is determining Role Treatments. Here are the different role treatments:

Maintain (M): The role is providing constant satisfaction and will in the future. The time spent in the role is ideal—no need to make any changes.

Reduce (R): The role is not providing satisfaction. The time spent on it is too much or isn't providing an acceptable return of satisfaction. You want to reduce the percentage this role composes of your identity, along with the amount of time you dedicate to it.

Eliminate (E): The role does not provide satisfaction, or you believe it will not provide satisfaction in the future. You want to eliminate the role from your identity.

Increase (I): You are not spending enough time on the role, and believe in the future that it could provide you with a meaningful level of satisfaction.

New (N): The role is not in your current identity, but you want it included. This could be a new pursuit that you think could be fun or revisiting a collaborative role (e.g., relationship) that may have been previously diminished or eliminated.

You can use the Current R-I Mapping, Future R-I Mapping, and Role Identity Action Planning Worksheet in Appendix C to capture your Role Treatments.

Step 6: Define Role Target Percentages for Your Future Identity

In your last two steps, you defined category target percentages and role treatments. Use this as a guide to now determine target percentages for each of your future roles. Put a target percentage next to each role and ensure that the total for each category aligns with the target percentages you set in your chart in Step 4.

You can use the Current R-I Mapping, Future R-I Mapping, and Role Identity Action Planning Worksheet in Appendix C to capture your Target Percentages.

Exhibit E: Future Role Identity Mapping Worksheet (Steps 5 and 6)

STEP 1	STEP 2	STEP 3	STEP 5	STEP 6
Role in Life	% Current Contribution to Positive Identity	% Time Spent	Role Treatment	Target % Contribution to Positive Identity & Time
Collaborative Roles				
Parent	15%	7%	Increase	20%
Spouse	10%	3%	Increase	13%
Friend	10%	3%	Increase	13%
Child	6%	2%	Increase	10%
Brother	4%	1%	Increase	6%
Coach	3%	3%	Maintain	3%
Volunteer	7%	1%	Increase	10%
Self-Centered Roles				
Industry (Famous/Powerful) Leader	10%	15%	Eliminate	0%
Wealthy Person	10%	25%	Reduce	2%
Beautiful Person	10%	15%	Reduce	5%
Life-Supporting Roles				
Wage Earner	5%	10%	Eliminate	0%
Hygienic Person	5%	1%	Increase	5%
Mentally/Emotionally Stable Person	5%	1%	Increase	5%
Healthy/Physically Fit Person	0%	0%	New	5%
Passive Roles				
Commuter	0%	4%	Eliminate	0%
Chore Provider	0%	7%	Eliminate	0%
Shopper	0%	6%	Reduce	3%
			TOTAL Collaborative	75%
			TOTAL Self-Centered	7%
			TOTAL Life-Supporting	15%
			TOTAL Passive	3%

Chapter Eight

Part III:
Role-Identity (R-I)
Action Planning

Step 7a: Target Roles for Immediate Action

Getting to your future identity will take time to happen. The best roles to target for action first are either the ones that require the most percentage change or the ones that you desire to have or not have in your life immediately. The first method will provide the most significant impact, while the second (if the percentage change is less) will provide the best chance for immediate progress. There is no correct method; the choice is up to you.

Step 7b: Define Activities That Will Move You Toward Your Goals and Eliminate Activities That Hold You Back

Our satisfaction in our roles is achieved through action, by performing activities that will propel us toward our goals. In your plan to move forward, you must reflect and document the activities in each of your roles. You must then assess if you are performing suitable activities. If you want to reduce or eliminate a role in your life, you could find ways to spend less time on that role.

As you examine your current activities, you can define positive ones that you are currently doing and keep doing them, eliminate harmful activities that are counterproductive to your goals, and add new activities that could propel you toward them. For collaborative roles, this could be seeing someone more or dedicating more time to them. If you want to be physically healthier, you could set up an exercise or nutrition program. To reduce time spent in passive roles, you can look for ways to do them quicker or transfer them to other people.

You can use the Current R-I Mapping, Future R-I Mapping, and Role Identity Action Planning Worksheet in Appendix C to capture your Activities.

Chapter Nine

Part IV: Role-Identity (R-I) Evaluation and Monitoring

A fter we set up our Action Plan, it is essential to monitor our progress toward our Future Identity. In this part of the process, we set up our Role-Identity Evaluation and Monitoring. We then can evaluate our satisfaction with our roles periodically (e.g., weekly) to assess how fulfilled we are in each one. **This part of the process can also immediately be used to evaluate your current satisfaction with your roles.** As I mentioned in the chapter on self-reflection, I used this process to provide myself an evaluation of where I derived my self-worth and found that I was not achieving as much current satisfaction as I thought from my self-centered work roles. It provided a strong impetus for me to make the change to stop working.

Step 8: Establish Your Role Evaluation Criteria, Evaluation Scale, and Total Identity Calculation

To perform an evaluation, we need Role Evaluation Criteria. We are documenting criteria to evaluate our level of satisfaction for each role. For example, for my parent role, I evaluated how fulfilled I was by how much quality time I spent with my children, the feedback I got from them about our time together, and their ability to manage themselves.

Here are some additional examples of evaluation criteria that I used:

Role in Life	Evaluation Criteria
Employee	Feeling like I made a difference; appreciation of my work by others via promotions, bonuses, awards, and raises
Financially Successful Person	Total wealth and performance over time
Healthy Person	Health indicators (weight, BMI, cholesterol, blood pressure), no health problems, overall feeling of physical wellness
Spouse, Child, Friend, Sibling	Share quality time, experiences, and pursuits, feelings of happiness and having a special connection, feeling appreciated
Coach	How much fun the kids are having, teamwork and skill development, positive feedback from the kids
Volunteer	Feeling that I am providing something of value to help others; the camaraderie of sharing a pursuit with others like me
All Passive Roles	Complete as quickly as possible to a satisfactory standard. Do not allow negative interactions to bother me

Once we have our criteria defined, we are ready to set our evaluation rating scale for each one.

Specifically, I set my scale for satisfaction from 0 to 5. Your scale can be whatever you would like. I just found this easiest for me. The better or more satisfied I felt, the higher (toward 5) I scored.

I finished my worksheet by putting in an overall identity calculation which was calculated by taking the role percentage multiplied by the rating for each role and then adding all of the ratings together. The formula is as follows:

(Role A Rating x Role A Percentage) + (Role B Rating x Role B Percentage), etc. = Total (Identity) Score.

Once you have completed these steps, you are ready to evaluate yourself. I did this weekly or any time a significant shift happened in a role. The more evaluations or data points, the better. It helps you see trends and gain meaningful insights about satisfaction in each role.

You can see an example of a R-I Evaluation and Monitoring Worksheet in Appendix C. Ideally you should setup your own spreadsheet for scoring yourself.

Step 9: Evaluate Your Role Satisfaction and Time Spent in Each Role

Based on your evaluation criteria, you can now score yourself on your level of satisfaction with each of your roles. I found it to be most effective to evaluate myself on a weekly basis. In addition to scoring yourself, you should capture the following for each role:

- Current positive activities that are contributing to satisfaction with the role

- Problems that are decreasing your score (detracting from your satisfaction with the role)

- Time spent

By understanding what is contributing to or detracting from your satisfaction with your roles, you can do the following to improve the satisfaction in your roles:

- Increase or decrease the time spent in that particular role

- Change the activities you are doing in that role

- Brainstorm new activities that could increase satisfaction or eliminate problems

Step 10: Monitor and Repeat

As you score yourself, you are ensuring that you are moving in the right direction towards your Future Identity Mapping. In other words, you are looking for increasing scores and eventually reaching a scoring goal to maintain. Your latest score is essentially your Current R-I Mapping.

The R-I Process is continuous. As you continue to monitor yourself, you will identify roles that you want to change and you will revisit and repeat the steps in Future R-I Mapping and R-I Action Planning.

Appendix A: Income, Expenses, and Retirement Age

The first critical part of understanding how much money is enough is determining what your total expenses are. Understanding your current expenses is reasonably straightforward; you know what you spend and can add in an extra calculation for unexpected costs. Through this exercise, you may also identify expenses for items or activities that do not bring you value or that you can eliminate or reduce.

The next group of expenses I put in my spreadsheet were those for future expenses like my children's college and future home improvements. I first projected a total expense. Then, I determined when the expense would occur. For example, I figured that the total college cost per child was $300,000, which would start being incurred as an expense in 10 years or 120 months. So, I had 10 years to save. My monthly cost per child was, therefore, $2,500 a month if I wanted to pay for all of college. I reduced the amount based on scholarships and student loans. The overall goal of this calculation is to have an idea of how much you will spend over the rest of your life.

The next part of my spreadsheet was determining my income over the rest of my life. I looked at how much I was saving per month (income - expenses). While working, my income included my salary and any investment income. After I retired, I would only have investment income along with any pension or social security. Keep in mind that this was in the aggregate. So, I looked at my income over my entire expected remaining life.

In the end, I had a financial spreadsheet that allowed me to either change the amount of money needed to retire or the age to retire. I found that age was indeed the driving factor, not money. As I said above, we work so we can spend time with the people and on the pursuits we love. The quicker we can get to that, the better. This part of the spreadsheet is essential. I modeled ages with how much money I required to retire. I identified a financial finish line and saw the age I would be at when I reached it. I was also able to reduce expenses and see the time reduced to get to retirement.

Others who used the spreadsheet could now clearly see the assumptions they had made on how much money they needed to retire would force them to work to a very old age (i.e., remember the retirement ages of 75 to 130?!) This immediate realization of how absurd and impossible this was led them back to reality to calculate a reasonable and attainable retirement age and savings.

Please note that there are a number of ways to cut unneeded expenses, budget, save more, get paid more, and invest better. I am no expert, but there certainly are people who are, and they have written thousands of books on those topics.

Appendix B: Helping Children to Live Purpose-Built Lives

I look at my job as a parent as guiding my children to be self-sufficient and capable of having meaningful, collaborative relationships and purpose. We need to give them time, guidance, and love now and build those relationships on the basis of our love and caring rather than on monetary support.

As I said earlier, it is a shame that, as children, we are taught to shift from being collaborative and relationship-driven to competitive and success-driven. It is better to teach children that instead of giving up those relationships for success, they should never give them up to start. They can sample success but should always focus on the people that truly matter.

We can teach them that when we try to cram everything into our lives, we become tired and do things halfway. When we do this, we have little time to form truly meaningful relationships.

I have always hated the phrase, *"I don't have time for that."*

How we spend our time is our choice. When we say this to someone, we are telling that person we are not important enough to make time for them and that they are not a priority in our lives. We must make time for those relationships and roles that are valuable to us, not make them wait until we are ready.

We must teach them that although they will experience competitive failure and have disappointments with people, they cannot look at everyone as bad and that they should avoid them. We must be there to support them. Children desperately crave relationships to counteract the fear that they are flawed people and, therefore, no one will love them. When they are having problems with their self-worth, they need reassurance that somebody somewhere finds them likable. You can be that person for them—to help them navigate the ups and downs of what they and other people do in the world. You can collaboratively guide them—showing them ways that they can feel whole by making a difference in others' lives.

Appendix C: Role-Identity (R-I) Worksheets

P lease use the three worksheets to complete the steps in the Roles Identity (R-I) Process. They include the following:

1. Role List

2. Current R-I Mapping, Future R-I Mapping, and Role Identity Action Planning Worksheet

3. R-I Evaluation and Monitoring Worksheet

Role List	
Role Name	**Role Type** (Collaborative, Self-Centered, Life-Supporting, Passive)

Current R-I Mapping, Future R-I Mapping, and Role Identity Action Planning Worksheet							
STEP 1	STEP 2	STEP 3	STEP 5	STEP 6		STEP 7b	
Role in Life	% Current Contribution to Positive Identity	% Time Spent	Role Treatment	Target (%) Positive Identity & Time	Current Positive Activities to Keep	New Activities to Consider (or Goals/Timeframes for Self-Centered Roles)	Current Negative Activities to Eliminate
Collaborative Roles							
Self-Centered Roles							
Life-Supporting Roles							
Passive Roles							
					NOTES		
TOTAL Collaborative							
TOTAL Self-Centered							
TOTAL Life-Supporting							
TOTAL Passive							

Role Identity Evaluation and Monitoring Worksheet

Role in Life	STEP 5 Role Treatment	STEP 6 Target (%) Postitive Identity and Time	STEP 8 Evaluation Definition	STEP 9 Current Positive Activities	New Activities That Could Help Improve Your Rating	Problems That Are Decreasing Your Rating	Week of (Date) Rating	Hours Spent	Week of (Date) Rating	Hours Spent
Collaborative Roles										
Self-Centered Roles										
Life-Supporting Roles										
Passive Roles										

NOTES

Total Score
Total Possible Score
% of Possible Score
Change from Previous Date

Acknowledgments

It has been over three years since I completed the first draft of my book. From inception through the journey to final delivery, I was inspired by memories, events, and people whom I would like to acknowledge.

My family, friends, and mentees have been very supportive of my writing journey. They have read and given feedback to one of my over fifty drafts. Their focus and willingness to help me see this book through has taken genuine wherewithal and commitment. I thank them for their honest feedback and unwavering support.

My mentees have been open to listening and trying the concepts in my book and worksheets. I greatly appreciate them trusting me. They told me it has really made a difference in how they think and live. It has brought me great happiness to know I have made a difference.

Lastly, I would like to thank my late father for his constant inspiration. His memory inspires me every day. My mother has carried on his memory. Her intelligence, humor, and level-headedness have guided me all my life.

Notes

www.ingramcontent.com/pod-product-compliance
Lightning Source LLC
Chambersburg PA
CBHW051130160726

47997CB00018B/1085